Space

UNITS 47, 48 STORYBOOK

ISBN 1-59318-510-3

10 09 08 07   4 5 6

SOPRIS WEST™ EDUCATIONAL SERVICES
A CAMBIUM LEARNING COMPANY

BOSTON, MA • LONGMONT, CO

A Problem in a Backpack

Planning Assistance: See Daily Lesson Planning for scheduling.

UNIT 48 • Space Facts

Space Is Vast

Planning Assistance: See Daily Lesson Planning for scheduling.

Space School

By Jerry Oltion
Illustrated by Fabricio VandenBroeck

Vocabulary Words

alien
An alien is a living thing that is not from around here. To people from Earth, an alien would be a living thing that is not from Earth.

asteroid
An asteroid is a rock in space that circles the Sun.

rescue ball
A rescue ball is an inflatable ball that can hold air and a person in an emergency. A rescue ball is like a space lifeboat.

space shuttle
A space shuttle is a spacecraft that moves people and things around in space.

space station
A space station is a spacecraft that can stay in space for a long time. People can live in a space station.

Try defining the next word. Then, look the word up in the glossary.

rescue
A rescue is when someone is . . .

UNIT 47 STORY

A Problem in a Backpack

A Problem in a Backpack

Look at the picture. Predict what the story will be about.

INTRODUCTION

If you look into the sky as far as you can see, you are looking out into space. Since the beginning of time, people have looked into space and wondered what is out there.

This story is about children who live and go to school in space. It takes place in the future. Is the story fact or fiction?

CHAPTER 1
The Problem

Maria stood on tiptoe to see over the heads of her classmates. They were all standing in line at the space station's airlock, waiting for a shuttle. They were going to take a field trip to the asteroid mine. Maria was waiting for her friend Asha. Where could she be? Asha loved asteroids. She wouldn't miss this field trip for anything!

The hall echoed with voices as the other kids talked about the shuttle ride. Everyone was excited. Maria wondered if the teacher would let her call Asha to ask where she was. Maria was just going to ask when Asha came hurrying up with her backpack in her hands.

"You're late!" Maria said. "We're about to leave."

Asha smiled, leaned close, and whispered in Maria's ear. "I had a little problem. In fact, I still have it!" Then, Asha giggled.

Where do the children live? Who are the main characters? Where is the class going? What is an asteroid?

How do you feel when you have a problem? Let's read the last paragraph again. As you read, listen for a clue about Asha's problem.

Asha seems happy about having a problem. In the next chapter, you'll find out three things—what the problem was, why Asha was happy about her problem, and something funny about the teacher.

CHAPTER 2

Asha's Secret

What happened in Chapter 1? Can you predict what Asha's secret is?

Asha was late to school on the day of the big field trip. Asha had told Maria that she was late because of a problem, but Asha had sounded excited. From her voice, Maria knew Asha wasn't in trouble. What else could she mean? Maria asked, "Why are you so happy about a problem?"

"Because nobody has ever caught one before," Asha said.

"Caught one? How could you catch a problem? Unless . . ."

Asha could only mean one thing. Small aliens had appeared on the space station a few weeks ago. Nobody knew where they had come from, but the little animals were getting into everything.

"You caught a problem?" Maria asked.

Asha flashed a big smile and grinned.

Maria squealed. "Really? Can I see it?"

"Keep your voice down!" Asha whispered. "If the teacher finds out, it'll take it away."

Maria looked around. There were fifty kids and only one teacher. Their teacher was an old worn-out model. Its metal body was dented and rusted with age.

It was too busy getting the kids ready for the field trip to notice Maria and Asha's excitement.

Look at the picture. Why did Maria call her teacher "it" instead of "he" or "she"? Describe the teacher.

CHAPTER 3

A Sneaker Snack

Who are the main characters? What is Asha's problem? Why doesn't Asha want her teacher to know about the problem? What is unusual about the children's teacher?

"Why did you bring the problem to school if the teacher will take it away?" Maria asked.

Asha responded, "Where would I keep it? The aliens chew through everything. I put it in my backpack, so it wouldn't be a problem."

Maria wasn't sure that was very smart. Asha's air tank was in her backpack. If the problem chewed up the tank, Asha wouldn't have any air if she needed it.

"I gave it my shoe to eat," Asha said.

"Your sneaker?" Maria asked. "What if the alien doesn't like to eat shoes?"

Asha said, "It was eating them when I found it, so . . ." Asha shrugged.

Show me what Asha did. What does it mean when someone shrugs?

Just then, the robot teacher said, "It is time to go." One by one the kids went into the shuttle. Maria and Asha sat in the back so they could open Asha's backpack and look at the problem.

The problem was a wrinkly ball about the size of a grapefruit, with tentacles sticking out on all sides and a mouth almost as wide as its body. The shoe beside it was missing most of the heel. While the girls watched, the problem pulled part of the sneaker into its mouth. There was a crunching sound, and the problem grew a little fatter.

Close your eyes and imagine what the alien would look like. Describe the alien. Now look at the picture on the next page. Why are the aliens a problem for the space station? Why is it a problem for Asha to have the problem in her backpack? In the next chapter, you'll find that the problem gets bigger!

CHAPTER 4
A Bigger Problem

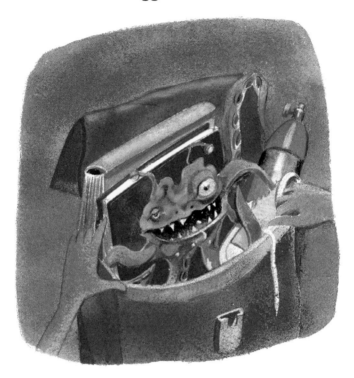

The problem in Asha's backpack was having a wonderful meal of Asha's sneaker. "What are you going to do when it finishes your shoes?" Maria asked.

"I hadn't thought about that," Asha said.

Look at the problem. Do you think it will cause any problems on the field trip?

The shuttle left the station, and the teacher started talking about the asteroid mine they were going to see. Asha and Maria tried to listen, but Maria heard a metal screech from Asha's pack. Maria looked into the backpack. The problem had grown! The shoes were gone, and it was working on the air tank.

Maria nudged Asha in the ribs and pointed into her pack. Asha's eyes grew wide. She grabbed for the tank, but the problem wrapped its tentacles around the tank and shoved it into its mouth. In one loud gulp, the air tank was gone!

"What do we do now?" Asha asked.

"I don't know," said Maria. "The problem is bigger, but it's still all wrinkly. I don't think it's full yet!"

"I noticed that too," gulped Asha. Then her voice got louder. "What are we going to do?"

This sounds dangerous. What do you think the girls should do?

"What do we do about what?" the teacher asked. It stretched its neck out across the length of the shuttle until its head was right in front of the two girls. Then it saw what was in Asha's pack.

What do you think will happen next?

CHAPTER 5

The Rescue Ball

Describe the problem. Explain how it has grown.

The girls were getting nervous. The problem was getting bigger, and the teacher had seen it. The teacher saw what was in Asha's pack and said, "You have a problem!"

Asha was too frightened to hide the problem. "It just ate my air tank!"

"Then I'm afraid we all have a problem," the teacher said. "It is just a matter of time before there is an explosion." Then the teacher calmly said, "Put your pack into the airlock."

"But the problem will die!" Asha cried.

The robot teacher said, "When the air tank explodes, the problem will die anyway." Then the robot teacher added, "And so will we."

How do you think Asha and Maria feel? Who needs a rescue?

Maria said, "We could put the problem in a rescue ball. Then maybe it would have a chance in space."

The teacher said, "That makes sense." It pulled a rescue ball off the wall and zipped it open. "Put your backpack in here," it said.

"What about my books and my music?" Asha asked.

Maria peered inside the backpack. "It ate those too," Maria said.

Asha pushed her backpack into the rescue ball. The teacher pulled a cord on the ball and it inflated with air. Then the teacher threw the ball into the airlock, closed the door, and pulled the handle. The airlock's outside door opened with a whoosh, and the rescue ball was blown out into space.

How did the teacher solve the problem? The problem is floating out in space inside the rescue ball. If you were on the space shuttle with the children, what would you do next? Read Chapter 6 to find out what happens to the problem.

CHAPTER 6

A Problem in Space

What has happened so far?

The rescue ball with the problem inside floated out into space. The whole class pressed up against the shuttle's windows. They could see the problem inside the ball. It ate the backpack. Then the problem stuck its mouth onto the rescue ball.

"Stop!" yelled Maria. Then the problem took a big bite out of the rescue ball. It split open and the air whooshed out. The problem floated into space.

"Oh no!" everyone groaned, but the problem just kept on eating. Before anyone could say anything else, the air tank exploded, and the problem puffed up like a big balloon.

The class watched in silence, but the problem seemed fine. It ate the last shreds of the rescue ball. The problem spun around a couple of times as if to say, "Thanks for lunch!" Then it zoomed off into space.

Maria spoke first, "Oh wow! Problems can live in space."

Asha said, "Maybe the problems can be sent back into space. Maybe they'd like that."

"Does that mean we won't have problems anymore?" Maria asked.

"Well, I know I don't," said Asha.

Just then, as if nothing had happened, the teacher announced, "The shuttle will soon arrive at the asteroid mine." With so much excitement, the class had forgotten about the field trip.

The problem had zoomed off into space. What do you think the problem will do next?

A PROBLEM IN A BACKPACK

◆ Who was the story about?
Where did the girls live?

● What happened at the beginning of the story?

■ What happened in the middle of the story?

▲ What happened at the end of the story?

Unit 47 Glossary

alien

An alien is a living thing that is not from around here. To people from Earth, an alien would be a living thing that is not from Earth.

asteroid

An asteroid is a rock in space that circles the Sun.

rescue

A rescue is when someone is saved from danger.

rescue ball

A rescue ball is an inflatable ball that can hold air and a person in an emergency. A rescue ball is like a space lifeboat.

Unit 47 Glossary (*continued*)

space shuttle

A space shuttle is a spacecraft that moves people and things around in space.

space station

A space station is a spacecraft that can stay in space for a long time. People can live in a space station.

Storybook Decoding Review

✏ **Sounds and words you can read:**

circle	knew	page	live
boat	point	road	city
oil	space	blue	voice

✈ **Words you can sound out:**

change	beside	know	asteroid
window	whispered	place	explosion
notice	rescue	problem	excitement

● **Words you can read:**

| almost | country | answer | against |
| question | field | love | wonder |

♥ **Phrases you can read:**

Go back to the drawing board.

Don't judge a book by its cover.

✏ **Sentences you can read:**

At the beginning, Asha had a problem in her backpack.

In the middle, the problem was eating and growing bigger.

At the end, the teacher sent the problem into space.

Space Facts

By Marilyn Sprick and Jerry Oltion

Vocabulary Words

astronaut
   An astronaut is a person who travels in space. The word "astronaut" comes from two very old words that mean "star" and "sailor."

atmosphere
   The atmosphere is the air that covers the Earth.

Earth
   Earth is a planet. We live on the planet Earth.

planet
   A planet is a large ball that circles a star. Earth is a planet.

star
   A star is a ball of glowing gas that planets sometimes circle around.

What We Think We Know

Space is a fascinating place. What do you think you already know about space?

What We'd Like to Learn

What would you like to learn about space?

UNIT 48 STORY

Space Is Vast

Space Is Vast

1. SPACE

"A Problem in a Backpack" is a fictional story that took place in space. Perhaps one day, you'll get to travel in space. Look at the headings. What will you find out in this section?

For as long as we can remember, people have looked up into the sky and dreamed of traveling in space. But what is space?

Earth and Space

Let's start with where we live. We live on the planet Earth. Earth is covered by a big, thick blanket of air. That blanket of air is called the Earth's atmosphere.

When you look past Earth's atmosphere at the Moon, the stars, and the Sun, you're looking into space. Space is big. No one knows exactly how big space is, but we do know this: Space is huge! Space is bigger than huge. Space is vast.

What does "vast" mean? Look back at the second paragraph. It says that Earth is covered by a thick blanket of air. What is that blanket of air called?

Look at the picture. Touch Earth. If
you travel away from Earth, the atmosphere
gets thinner and thinner until there is no air.
Everything beyond that is space. Touch space.

Earth and the Solar System

Beyond Earth is the Moon. Our Moon circles the Earth, and Earth is one of nine planets that circle the Sun.

Our Sun, its planets, and the moons that travel around each planet are called the Solar System.

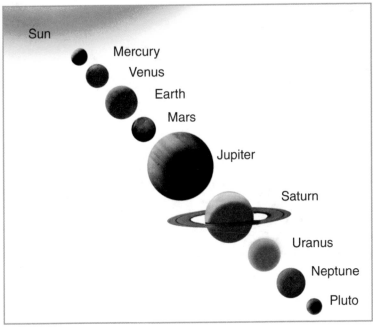

This picture shows the order of the planets. Touch the Sun. The first planet from the Sun is Mercury. Touch Mercury. The second planet is Venus. Touch Venus. The third planet is Earth. Touch Earth. Describe Earth.

2. THE EARTH AND THE MOON

Life on Earth

Look at the picture. It shows what Earth looks like from space. Much of Earth is covered by water. From space, water looks blue. Trace the places where water is covering the Earth. Then trace the places where there is land.

Why does Earth look blue from space? If you aren't sure, look back on page 31.

Earth is made up of water and land. We also know that Earth is covered with a blanket of air. As far as we know, living things need air and water. Earth has both! What about the Moon? Do you think people could live on the Moon?

Exploring on the Moon

Our Moon circles the Earth. For as long as we can remember, people have dreamed of traveling to the Moon.

Did you know that twelve people have been to the Moon? The first people to walk on the Moon were two American astronauts—Neil Armstrong and Buzz Aldrin. It took the astronauts three days to travel to the Moon, and then it took one more day to land.

If you got to walk on the Moon, what would you say?

I think I would say "WOW!" What would you say?

When Neil Armstrong took his first step on the Moon, he said, "That's one small step for man, one giant leap for mankind."

Living on the Moon

Scientists knew there would be no air on the Moon. Look at the picture of the astronaut walking on the moon. What was he wearing? The astronaut's backpack had air tanks.

The Moon has no air and no large amounts of water. Scientists have found that the Moon is a big ball of rock with no life. Would you like to live on the Moon?

3. TRAVELING IN SPACE

What facts do you know about the Moon? Would you like to live on the Moon? Let's look at the headings in this section. What are we going to learn about?

Traveling to the Moon

We know that landing on the Moon and returning to Earth safely is possible. That is very exciting! We also know that living on the Moon would be hard. People would have to take air, water, and food with them.

Living in Space

What about traveling to other planets? Scientists are learning new things about living and traveling in space. Did you know that there are astronauts living in space? That's right! There are people living in space.

The International Space Station

Astronauts are not living on another planet. That hasn't happened yet. Astronauts are living on the International Space Station.

In 1995, the United States, Canada, and fourteen other nations began working together to build the Space Station. Just like the Moon, the Space Station circles around Earth in space.

Touch the picture of the International Space Station. Who built the Space Station? How is the Space Station like the Moon?

The Space Station was very difficult to build. Think about it. Every piece of the station had to be carried into space—piece by piece.

Two to seven astronauts can live on the Space Station at one time. Each crew stays on the Space Station for many months before they return to Earth. The astronauts conduct experiments, take photos, make repairs, and even go on spacewalks! Would you like to live on a space station?

What do we know about space travel? What would you like to know about life on a space station? Would you like to be an astronaut or a scientist so you could explore space? In the next section, you are going to read about traveling to other planets.

4. TRAVELING TO OTHER PLANETS

For as long as we can remember, people have imagined traveling to the other planets. We've sent people to the Moon. We have people living on a Space Station, but no one has ever traveled to any other planet.

Space Probes

People can't travel to and from other planets yet. So, instead of sending people to other planets, scientists send spacecraft called probes.

This is a space probe. The space probe is called Voyager II. Voyager II visited four planets before leaving the Solar System.

Probes to Pluto

Let's look at the Solar System again.

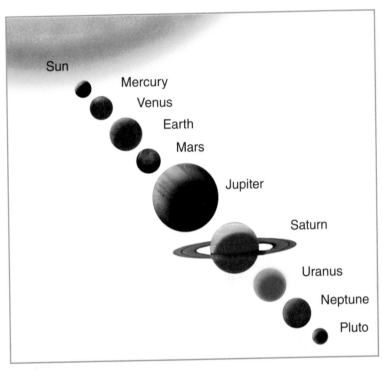

Find Earth. Now find the planet farthest from the Sun. That planet is Pluto. Probes have been sent to every planet in the Solar System except Pluto. Scientists are planning to send a probe to Pluto, but it is so far away it will take the probe about nine years to get there!

5. SURPRISES IN SPACE

What facts do you know about space travel so far? Scientists have learned a lot about space from probes and astronauts. In this section, we'll learn some surprising information that scientists learned about space using equipment from Earth. Let's read the headings to see what we'll learn about.

<u>Telescopes</u>

For as long as we can remember, people have looked at the Moon and the stars and dreamed of traveling in space. For about 400 years, people have studied space by looking through telescopes.

This is a picture of a telescope.

When you look through a telescope, things that are far away look closer. Do you know anyone who has a telescope?

Telescopes that scientists use are getting bigger and more powerful. These telescopes make it possible for scientists to look farther and farther into space.

Some telescopes are so big they need their own building.

Sedna

In 2003, using a telescope, scientists saw something new in our Solar System. It is three times farther away from the Sun than Pluto. It is round and red in color. It is very cold, and it circles the Sun every 10,000 years. Scientists have named it Sedna.

Scientists say that Sedna is like a planet, but scientists don't think Sedna should be called a planet. So, what is Sedna? Scientists don't know what it should be called!

Sedna has been a big surprise to many people, but not to many scientists. Scientists have guessed that there are other things in our Solar System that we don't know about yet. Scientists have many questions and many good guesses about what will be found in space.

What did scientists discover in 2003? Sedna is three times farther away than Pluto. It's going to take the space probe about nine years to get to Pluto. So, it would take a space probe at least 27 years to get to Sedna. If you could travel to Sedna, how old would you be when you got there?

6. THE STARS

What are some of the interesting facts we've learned about space? In this section we're going to learn more about the vastness of space. What does "vast" mean?

The Sun

Scientists are only beginning to learn about our Sun and the planets that circle it. Did you know that our Sun is a star? In fact, our Sun is just one of many stars.

Ten Billion Trillion

On a clear night, when we look out into space beyond the Earth's atmosphere, we can see about 2,000 stars without the help of a telescope. Using telescopes, scientists have learned that there are more stars in space than we can see.

Scientists think there are about ten billion trillion stars in space! Ten billion trillion is such a big number that it is almost impossible to imagine.

If you tried to count ten billion trillion stars, it would be like trying to count all the grains of sand on all the beaches on Earth. That's how many stars are in space.

Look at the stars. Let's see if we can list four facts we've learned about stars.

The Vastness of Space

Scientists have learned that there are about ten billion trillion stars, and they know that many of the stars have planets that circle them.

So, what do we know about space? Space is big. Space is huge! Space is bigger than huge. Space is vast!

In the Future

Scientists are learning more about space every day. Perhaps one day, you could take a vacation in space. Perhaps one day, there will be space cities and space schools.

Perhaps one day, we may learn that there are aliens living in space. What do you think?

Unit 48 Glossary

alien

> An alien is a living thing that is not from around here. To people from Earth, an alien would be a living thing that is not from Earth.

astronaut

> An astronaut is a person who travels in space. The word "astronaut" comes from two very old words that mean "star" and "sailor."

atmosphere

> The atmosphere is the air that covers the Earth.

Earth

> Earth is a planet. We live on the planet Earth.

planet

A planet is a large ball that circles a star. The Earth is a planet.

Solar System

The Solar System is the Sun and all the planets and other objects that circle the sun.

space probe

A space probe is a spacecraft that carries equipment to explore space. A space probe does not carry people.

star

A star is a ball of glowing gas that planets sometimes circle around.

vast

Vast means very large—bigger than huge. Space is vast.

Storybook Decoding Review

Sounds and words you can read:

caution	noise	engine	phone
toad	photo	voice	fault
giraffe	road	haul	imagine

Words you can sound out:

nation	those	silence	giant
know	unsafe	reglue	possible
these	difficult	system	fantastic

Words you can read:

certain	caught	through	special
front	either	both	clothes

Phrases you can read:

Don't judge a book by its cover.

Better late than never.

Sentences you can read:

Our Sun is one of many stars out in space.

Earth is one of nine planets that circle the Sun.

Our Moon circles around Earth.